ABOUT THE AUT[HOR]

Portrait by Rafael Maniago

A former student of Donna Dewberry and several other top decorative artists, Jan Belliveau's decorative painting career now spans 30 years. Today, she is an accomplished painter and teacher, working out of her Temecula, California, studio and store, The Painting Goose. A former East coast resident, Jan owned a successful painting studio in Turnersville, New Jersey, for 12 years.

Jan is a member of "Anonymous Painters," a chapter of the Society of Decorative Painters (SDP). She teaches at SDP conventions held across the country, and is a regular exhibitor at the Creative Painting Convention in Las Vegas.

Together with her husband, Bill, and granddaughter, Aislynn, Jan now resides in Murrieta, California, where she enjoys sunshine almost year round.

DEDICATION

This book is dedicated to the students of the former Jan's Folk Art Studio in Turnersville, New Jersey. These students, who quickly became friends, gave me the confidence to push my limits. They will always be in my heart. I'd also like to dedicate this book to my husband, Bill, who has always encouraged me to follow my dreams. He has been most supportive in each endeavor, whether it be at the scroll saw, balancing the books or putting up with my traveling.

ACKNOWLEDGMENTS

I would like to give a special thanks to my business partner, Leslie Hokeness, who put up with my taking so much time off to get this book completed, and at the same time keeping my coffee cup full.

SOURCES

Brushes
Black Gold by
Dynasty
www.dynasty-brush.com

Paint, Mediums, Varnishes
Ceramcoat
Delta Technical Coatings
www.deltacrafts.com

Clock (page 12)
Walnut Hollow
www.walnuthollow.com

Craft stores carry a wide variety of supplies. If you need something special, ask your local store to contact the listed companies. Some of the products featured in this book may be ordered from:
The Painting Goose
28780 Old Town Front St.
Temecula, CA 92590
www.thepaintinggoose.com

CREDITS

Produced by
Banar Designs, Inc. / P.O. Box 483 / Fallbrook, CA 92088
email: banar@earthlink.net
www.banardesigns.com

Art Direction: Barbara Finwall
Editorial Direction: Nancy Javier
Photography: Stephen Whalen
Computer Graphics: Wade Rollins and Chris Nelsen
Project Direction: Jerilyn Clements
Writing: Susan Borsch
Editing: Jerilyn Clements, Nancy Javier, Victoria Dye
Pattern Illustrations and Project Testing: Victoria Dye

07 06 05 04 03 5 4 3 2 1   ISBN 1-58180-464-4

TABLE OF

CONTENTS

JAN'S SUPPLY LIST

Brushes

I use the Black Gold line of brushes from Dynasty. You may wish to narrow down this list to an assortment of brushes you're most comfortable with.

⅝-inch (15mm) flat shader (206G)

nos. 1, 2, 4, 6, 8, 10, 12, 14, 16 flat shaders (206S)

nos. 4, 6 rounds (206R)

nos. 1, 2 liners (206L)

nos. 8, 12 waves (206WV)

Scruffy brush (any worn brush)

⅝-inch (15mm) flat shader

no. 16 flat shader

no. 14 flat shader

no. 12 flat shader

no. 10 flat shader

no. 8 flat shader

no. 6 flat shader

no. 4 flat shader

no. 2 flat shader

no. 1 flat shader

no. 6 round

no. 1 liner

no. 0 liner

no. 12 wave

no. 8 wave

scruffy brush

Paint

Delta Ceramcoat acrylics are my favorite paints. They have a wide variety of colors so mixing paints isn't as necessary. They also have a rich, creamy consistency and offer great coverage.

Paint Mediums

I like Delta Color Float for blending, shading and linework. For extending the drying time of paint, I use Delta Gel Blending Medium. Follow the manufacturer's instructions for using them.

Palette Knife

I prefer a metal palette knife with an angled shaft, which makes moving paint puddles easier. It's also more durable than a plastic one.

Sanding Pads

For sanding wood pieces, I use a fine-grit sanding pad. They are more durable than sandpaper, they hold their shape and they make it easier to sand hard-to-reach areas. They also hold up very well for wet sanding.

Brush Basin

A brush basin is filled with water for cleaning brushes. Most have three compartments: one for swishing off the excess paint, one with a grid for vibrating the paint off the ferrule, and the third for storing clean water in order to do side loading.

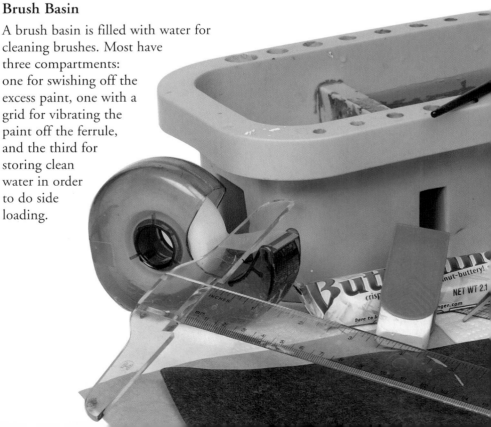

Wet Palette

A wet palette keeps your paint moist while painting. I make my own wet palette. I use a thin plastic pencil box (available from stationery stores) lined with a piece of chamois cloth cut to fit. Then I cut a piece of deli wrap (available in grocery supply stores). Cover your wet palette when you're finished painting and your paints will still be fresh the next day.

Palette Paper

I prefer gray palette paper, which is available in tear-off pads. I keep a piece next to my wet palette for mixing paint and to stroke paint-loaded brushes.

Stylus

A stylus is used to transfer your pattern from the tracing paper to your surface. A stylus has two points, one on each end. The stylus can also be dipped in paint and used to create dots.

Eraser

I use a Factis extra soft white eraser.

GENERAL INSTRUCTIONS

Cotton Swabs

To make corrections, I use a moistened cotton swab to lightly erase or remove mistakes. These can also be used for lifting excess paint or for making fluffy dots.

Marking Pen

For tracing patterns, use a Sharpie permanent marker with an ultra fine point. I like this pen because it doesn't smear and is permanent.

Other Supplies

Delta All-Purpose Sealer
Delta Exterior/Interior brush-on varnish
Delta Faux Finish Glaze Base, clear
Delta Crackle Medium
Delta Candle & Soap Painting Medium
Delta Brush Cleaner
Paper towels
Tracing paper
Graphite paper
Scotch Magic tape
Sea sponge
1-inch (25mm) foam brush
Pencil and sharpener
Ruler
Craft knife
Scissors

Transferring the Design

Lay the tracing paper over the pattern and trace it carefully with the marking pen (I use a Sharpie). Then place the tracing paper over a piece of graphite paper (white or gray) graphite-side down on the object. Trace over the lines with a stylus using light pressure. Check your lines as you're tracing and make any adjustments.

Mixing Colors

In this book, when instructed to mix paints, the proportion is 1:1 unless otherwise stated. When proportions of paint are different, it will be indicated, such as 2:1, which means two parts of the first color and one part of the next. If paint is to be double-loaded, the colors will be listed as, "Double load with Sonoma Wine and Sachet Pink."

Caring for Brushes

When you purchase a new brush, clean it in water to remove any sizing. After using brushes, always clean them with a brush cleaner. Rinse with water and dry the brush on a paper towel, then reshape the bristles. Never let paint dry in the brush and never let brushes soak in water.

Basecoating

This means applying a smooth coat of paint over your surface. This will be the background of your design. For large pieces, use a foam brush or roller. For smaller pieces, use a wash brush.

Varnish

Two to three coats of exterior/interior varnish protects your beautifully painted pieces. Sand between coats. You may select a matte, semi-gloss or high-gloss varnish.

BRUSHSTROKES

Side Loading: 1. Clean a flat brush in water. Blot off excess water. Dip one side of brush into a fresh puddle of paint on the palette. Blend brush back and forth in the same spot at least five times to remove excess paint.

2. Paint will float gradually across the brush. Do not allow it to reach the other side. Remember that the wider the brush, the easier it is to side load.

Walking a Side Load: Load the brush as in Side Loading step 1. Stroke the brush as in side loading, moving the brush slowly in the direction of the fade. Moving the brush too quickly will leave stripes (as shown at top).

Double Loading: Dip one side of the brush into one color of paint. Dip the other side into a second color. Stroke brush back and forth in the same spot until the two colors are blended in the center.

S-Stroke: 1. Using either a flat shader or a liner of your choice, load brush (flatten liner while loading). Start on the chisel at a 45° angle.

2. Then pull the brush to the left, flatten to the right and lift to a chisel edge to the left. S-strokes should start and end at 45° angles.

C-Stroke: Fully load a flat shader. Starting with the brush in a horizontal position, paint a "C." Do not let the brush twist between your fingers. The stroke should go from thin to thick to thin.

Closed C-Stroke: With the loaded brush on a 45° angle, let the top of the brush twist from a 10:00 position to a 2:00 position, pushing up slightly at the 10:00 and pulling in slightly at the 2:00.

Comma Strokes: 1. Load any size liner with paint, flattening the bristles while loading. The larger the liner brush, the larger the comma will be.

2. Press the brush down and pull toward you, lifting pressure as you pull. Comma strokes have a slight curve.

Slip-Slap: Using a fully loaded flat shader, wipe excess paint on a paper towel. Make loose x's in a slip-slap motion to fill in area desired.

Stipple: Using a scruffy brush, dip brush into paint and pounce excess onto a paper towel. Gently tap desired area to get a light and lacy look.

BRUSHSTROKES

One-Stroke Leaf: 1. Using a fully loaded or double-loaded brush, set the brush down, press and twist. Lift pressure on the brush gradually as you twist.

2. Twist the brush slightly and end on the chisel of the brush (the tip of the bristles).

B-Stroke: With a loaded flat brush at a 45° angle, let the brush twist from a 10:00 position to a 2:00 position, dipping in at the center. Continue the stroke to form a point.

Two-Stroke Leaf: Hold a fully loaded or double-loaded brush in a vertical position. Twist it between thumb and finger from 12:00 position to the 6:00 position, letting the brush flair out at 4:00. Do the same in mirror image on the opposite side.

Plaid: Use a fully loaded wave brush. With a light touch, stroke brush across area in one direction, then in the other direction.

Linework: Thin paint to the consistency of ink. Hold the loaded liner brush with the tip of the brush grazing the surface. Slowly move the brush on the surface by moving your whole arm instead of your wrist.

Consistent Dot: Dip the wooden end of your brush into a fresh puddle of paint and dot surface. In order for the dots to remain the same size, you must dip into the paint each time. The larger the brush, the larger the dot will be.

Set Downs: Using a fully loaded liner, set the bristles down creating an oval with the paint.

Tear Drop Stroke: Using a fully loaded liner brush, press and pull toward you, twisting and lifting the brush as you pull.

Note:

The word "float" is often used in the instructions. This refers to applying your paint with a side-loaded brush. It is usually used when shading or highlighting.

BRUSH LETTERING PRACTICE PAGE

1. Lay a piece of vellum or heavy tracing paper over this page. With a pencil and straight edge, draw the baseline and top line as shown in red.

2. Load a no. 1 flat shader with paint thinned slightly thicker than the consistency of ink. Pull the brush through the paint to load one side of the brush and then flip it over to load the other side. Pull the brush across the palette to evenly distribute the paint, then flip over and do it again, keeping a sharp chisel edge on the brush.

3. Hold the brush gently between your thumb and first finger with the handle resting on your middle finger, much like holding a pencil. Keep your hand firmly on the surface with your little finger extended.

4. Keep the chisel point of the brush at a 45º angle to the baseline. The entire chisel edge should touch the paper. In italics every stroke of every letter should begin and end at a 45º angle.

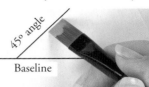

5. Turn the page so that you pull all strokes down and to the right. Never push the brush up or to the left.

6. Notice the red numbers and arrows on the letters below. Follow these to make your strokes. Most of the letters are made up of several strokes.

7. Practice until you feel confident to do the lettering on your chosen project.

Italic Brush Lettering

ABCDEFGHI
JKLMNOP
QRSTUVWX
YZ123456789

abcdefghijklmn
opqrstuvwxyz

POETRY PEBBLES

Love is the Poetry Heart Create in your Joy Beaut

Blue Wisp

Pale Lilac

Stonewedge
Green

Dark Foliage
Green

POETRY PEBBLES

Since many people enjoy meditation, mood-setting candle gardens are now a popular home accessory. It's easy to put a "zen" candle garden together using a flat box, sand, a rake and smooth stones.

To personalize this gift, you can use your decorative painting skills to write a pretty word or name across each stone. Arrange the stones to form an uplifting message on the sand and then provide alternative words for your recipient to play with as she contemplates. One thing will be very clear…her appreciation for your creativity!

Supplies

Smooth stones (preferably flat)
Delta Exterior/Interior Varnish
Graphite paper

Brush

no. 1 flat

Transfer the pattern onto the stone using graphite paper—white for dark stones, gray for light stones. Paint the letters using a no. 1 flat and the color of your choice. Tip: On darker stones, it's best to use lighter colors, such as Blue Wisp or Pale Lilac.

To finish, apply a coat of varnish

ABCDEFGHIJKLMOPQ
RSTUVWXYZ1234567890

abcdefghijklmnopqrstuvwxyz

Poetry Peace Love Beauty Joy I Heart Always Create Harmony the and is for you your in be will my

Use the alphabet or words above to create your own poetry.

Other ideas for short quotes or poems:

The simplest objects are eternal...
            —Pierre Auguste Renoir

Heaven is under our feet
as well as over our hearts
            —Thoreau

The new-laid garden...
Rocks settling
In harmony
In soft winter rain
            —Shado

Clear colored stones
are vibrating in
the brook-bed...
or the water is
            —Soseki

The following are suggested quotes made up of the words shown above:

I will always love you

Poetry is in the heart

Create beauty love and joy

I will create beauty

Peace be in your heart

Create harmony

Love and beauty will create peace in your heart

You will always be in my heart

Display ideas:

• Spread smooth sand in a flat dish or tray, add candles. Scatter pebbles around candles, then rake the sand with a comb into swirling designs (as shown in the photo on page 9).

• Cement the pebbles onto the sides of garden pots to create mosaic designs.

• Make a garden path of cement and pebbles, scattering the painted poetry pebbles among them.

Light Ivory

 Autumn Brown

 Bambi Brown

 Cape Cod Blue

 Payne's Grey

 Lavender

SEIZE THE DAY

A small clock is always a nice gift, especially for a busy achiever with many appointments to keep. Whether placed on a desk top, bedroom dresser or bathroom counter, this painted, wooden clock is eye-catching and definitely makes a statement!

The use of color here is striking, and the lettering is also artfully placed, with one bold message calling out amidst an echoing sea of diagonal words. This is actually three thoughtful gifts in one: attractive decorative piece, functional clock and motivational day brightener!

Supplies

Wooden clock (Walnut Hollow)
Delta All-Purpose Sealer
Delta Exterior/Interior Varnish
Sanding pad, fine grit
Graphite paper, gray
Worn toothbrush
1-inch(25mm) foam brush

Brushes

⅝-inch (15mm) flat shader
nos. 2, 6, 12 flat shaders
no. 1 liner
Scruffy brush

Prep: Remove the clock face. Sand the wood using the fine grit sanding pad. Brush on Delta All-Purpose Sealer using a ⅝-inch (15mm) flat brush or 1-inch (25mm) foam brush.

1. Base the clock using the ⅝-inch (15mm) flat or 1-inch (25mm) foam brush and Light Ivory. Two coats may be necessary.

While still wet, go over the ivory with a ⅝-inch (15mm) flat and a watery wash of Autumn Brown (4 parts water to 1 part paint).

2. Use a no. 1 liner to float Bambi Brown on puddles of water here and there. In the same areas, stipple lightly using a no. 1 liner and Autumn Brown.

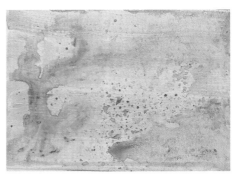

3. Flick your finger over a worn toothbrush to spatter over the piece with a watery mixture first of Autumn Brown and then Bambi Brown (2 parts water to 1 part each paint).

4. Paint the inner borders of the clock using a no. 12 flat and Cape Cod Blue. With the no. 6 flat, paint the outer borders with Lavender.

5. Trace the shape of the front and the base of the clock on a large piece of tracing paper. Position the lettering pattern (from page 46) on an angle and trace it repeatedly over the shapes of the clock. Transfer the pattern using graphite paper. Paint the light lettering with a no. 2 flat brush and Cape Cod Blue; paint the dark lettering with Payne's Grey.

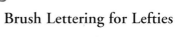

6. Paint the border of the clock face using a no. 6 flat and Cape Cod Blue. Allow to dry. Brush a coat of varnish onto the entire surface. Then return the clock face and works to the wood piece following the manufacturer's instructions.

Brush Lettering for Lefties

If you're left-handed, follow the instructions on page 8 except hold the brush in a mirror image of the way the right-handed person holds it. Swivel your paper 90° clockwise. Do not extend your little finger. You will be lettering from the top to the bottom of the page instead of from left to right.

EVERY DAY IS A GIFT

Candles are extremely popular now—good news for a decorative painter in search of a gift idea. You can decorate a candleholder and, for a perfect gift set, paint a pillar candle to coordinate with your design.

"Paintable" candleholders can be made of metal, wood, stoneware or papier mache, as in the sample shown. This one highlights a sweet, hand-lettered reminder to cherish each new day. Framed with pretty leaves and vines, the message stands out against a dark blue background.

Salem Blue

Stonewedge
Green

Blueberry

Dark Forest
Green

Light Ivory

Ivory

EVERY DAY IS A GIFT

Supplies

Papier mache box
Pillar candle, ivory
Delta Candle and Soap
  Painting Medium
Graphite paper, gray and
  white

Brushes

nos. 1, 6, 12 flat shaders
no. 1 liner

1. Base the inside of the box with Salem Blue using a no. 12 flat shader. Base the outside with Blueberry.

2. Transfer the pattern from pages 44-45 using white graphite paper.

3. Basecoat all the leaves with Stonewedge Green using a no. 6 flat. Stroke in vines using a no. 1 liner and Stonewedge Green.

4. Shade the base of the leaves using a no. 6 flat with a side load of Dark Forest Green. Using a no. 1 liner and Dark Forest Green, pull veins into the leaves and create shadow lines along the underside of the vines.

5. Create highlights on the leaves using a no. 6 flat with a side load of Light Ivory. Highlight the stems using a no. 1 flat shader with a sideload of Light Ivory.

6. Stroke letters (see page 8) using a no. 1 flat and Ivory.

7. Transfer the leaf pattern to the candle using gray graphite paper. Add a touch of Candle and Soap Painting Medium to Dark Forest Green mixed with Ivory (1:1). Paint the leaves using a no. 6 flat and vines using a no. 1 liner. Paint veins using a no. 1 liner and Dark Forest Green. Create shadow lines under the vines with the Dark Forest Green.

Blueberry

Lavender
Lace

Magnolia
White

Old
Parchment

Light Foliage
Green

Medium
Foliage Green

Dark Foliage
Green

Lavender

Rhythm 'N
Blue

MORNING GLORY PLAQUE

The turn of a phrase can be beautiful, in fact, even a work of art. Add calligraphy and some colorful paint, and such a meaningful message becomes the basis for a wonderful, personalized gift. An unfinished wooden plaque is your blank slate, awaiting a decorative touch and a sentimental saying just right for a certain someone.

Unlike a bottle of perfume, this is the type of timeless gift that endures throughout the years. The example here showcases a lovely garland of painted morning glories surrounding a message of Irish cheer. 'Tis lovely!

Supplies

Oval plaque (The Painting Goose)
Delta All-Purpose Sealer
Delta Satin Exterior/Interior Varnish
Delta Gel Blending Medium
Delta Float Color
Sanding pad, fine grit
Graphite paper, gray
Sea sponge, small piece
1-inch (25mm) foam brush

Brushes

⅝-inch (15mm) flat shader
nos. 1, 8, 12 flat shaders
no. 1 liner

Prep:

Sand any rough edges with a sanding pad.

Mix Old Parchment and All-Purpose Sealer (1:1) and base the plaque using a ⅝-inch (15mm) flat shader or 1-inch (25mm) foam brush. Sand again lightly. Paint a second coat of Old Parchment.

1. Paint the front of the plaque using the ⅝-inch (15mm) flat shader or 1-inch (25mm) foam brush and Gel Blending Medium. While wet, side load a float of Blueberry around the outer edge of the plaque using a no. 12 flat shader. Walk the color toward the center (see page 6), adding Lavender Lace as you go.

2. With a sea sponge, dab Blueberry on the first rim. Paint the outside rim Lavender with a no. 8 flat.

3. Transfer the basic pattern from page 45.

4. **Morning glories:** Basecoat all the morning glories using a no. 12 flat shader and Lavender.

Leaves: Using a no. 8 flat shader and Medium Foliage Green, basecoat all the leaves.

5. Side load a no. 12 flat shader with Rhythm 'N Blue and place a float on either side of each star in the morning glories. With a no. 12 flat shader, side load a float of Dark Foliage Green at the base of the leaves. Create veins in each leaf using a no. 1 liner and Dark Foliage Green, forming an S-stroke (see page 6).

6. Using no. 1 liner and Blueberry, fill in the star.

7. Side load a no. 12 flat shader and float Lavender Lace on the outer edges of the morning glory in between the star areas.

Side load a no. 12 flat shader with Light Foliage Green and float a highlight on the top edges of each leaf.

8. Using a no. 12 flat shader and Magnolia White, place a float of color around the center fading out.

9. Using a small scruffy brush and Old Parchment, dab in the center of the flower. While wet, tap in Dark Foliage Green without cleaning the brush.

10. Load a no. 1 liner with Dark Foliage Green thinned to an inky consistency and line in stems and vines.

11. Stroke in the lettering (see page 8) using a no. 1 flat shader and Rhythm 'N Blue. Finish by brushing on a coat of varnish.

WISH FRAME

A gift that's truly unforgettable is one that is very, very personal. A meaningful photograph framed in a special way can be just the right thing for a friend or loved one, and only someone very close would know.

Your decorative painting skills can help you create a one-of-a-kind frame worthy of the priceless picture inside. With a plaid background and tiny, decorative blossoms, this frame is very pretty. And the added wording really makes it special. Each time a mother looks at this gift her heart will overflow again.

Moss Green

Wedgwood Green

Deep Lilac

Eggplant

White

Phthalo Blue

Dark Forest Green

Spice Brown

Old Parchment

Blue Wisp

WISH FRAME

Supplies

Wooden frame
Delta All-Purpose Sealer
Delta Exterior/Interior Varnish
Sanding pad, fine grit
Ruler
Pencil
Graphite paper, gray
1-inch (25mm) foam brush

Brushes

nos. 1, 6 flat shaders
no. 1 liner
no. 8 wave

Prep: Sand the frame with a fine grit sanding pad. Apply the sealer using a 1-inch (25mm) foam brush. Basecoat the frame using the foam brush and Blue Wisp.

1. **Plaid:** Lightly draw in a grid of ¾" (2cm) squares using a ruler and pencil. Use a no. 8 wave brush and Old Parchment to paint the vertical lines of the grid. Stroke in a thin, straight line using a no. 1 liner and Old Parchment on the side of each line.

2. Repeat the same process for the horizontal lines.

3. Transfer the pattern from page 44 using graphite paper.

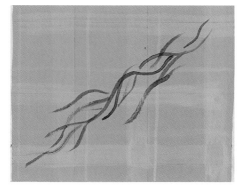

4. **Vines:** Paint the vines using a no. 1 liner and Spice Brown. Create variety by adding a few vines of Dark Forest Green.

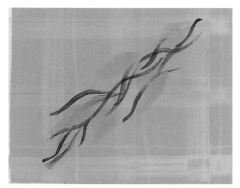

5. **Leaves:** Add one-stroke background leaves (see page 7) using a no. 6 flat and thinned Moss Green (2 parts water to 1 part paint).

6. Stroke in leaves using a no. 1 liner loaded with a mixture of Wedgwood Green and Moss Green (1:1). Add variety by shading some leaves with a no. 1 flat, side loaded with Dark Forest Green.

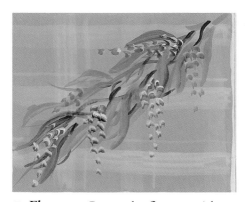

7. **Flowers:** Create the flowers with a no. 1 flat, double loaded with Deep Lilac and White. Make small C-strokes (see page 6) keeping the White at the top. Paint more flowers with a double load of Eggplant and White.

8. Stroke in the lettering (see page 8) using a no. 1 flat and Phthalo Blue.

9. Brush on a coat of varnish.

SOW SEEDS OF KINDNESS

Planting flower seeds is a joyful chore filled with expectation for the beautiful rewards to come. This painted wooden planter and three matching clay pots capture the glad mood and help create a perfect ensemble gift for an avid gardener.

The planter and pots are covered in a bed of green, then decorated with cheery polka dots. Purple blossoms also accent the container, along with a garden-themed inspirational message. This hand-painted gift would be a wonderful addition to any window box, deck or patio.

Forest Green

 Dark Jungle Green

 Purple Dusk

 Vintage Wine

 Custard

 White

 Butter Cream

 Village Green

 Eucalyptus

SOW SEEDS OF KINDNESS

Supplies

Wooden planter with handles
3 small terra-cotta pots
Sanding pad, fine grit
Delta All-Purpose Sealer
Delta Satin Exterior/Interior Varnish
Graphite paper, white
Stylus
1-inch (25mm) foam brush
Pencil with eraser

Brushes

nos. 1, 4, 8, 10 flat shaders
no. 1 liner

Prep:

Sand any rough edges using a fine grit sanding pad. Seal the entire piece using a 1-inch (25mm) foam brush and Delta All-Purpose Sealer. Sand a second time.

1. Basecoat the piece using the foam brush and Forest Green.

2. Allow to dry, then sand the edges of the piece with the sanding pad to give a worn appearance.

3. Transfer the pattern from pages 42–43 using graphite paper.

4. **Lettering:** Stroke in all lettering (see page 8) using Butter Cream and a no. 1 flat shader.

5. **Leaves:** Using a no. 8 flat shader, double load the brush with Village Green and Eucalyptus. Stroke in three two-stroke leaves (page 7). Double load the no. 1 liner by dragging through Village Green and Eucalyptus and line the vines. Shade with a no. 4 flat and a side load of Dark Jungle Green.

6. **Pansies:** Double load a no. 10 flat shader with Purple Dusk and Vintage Wine. Stroke in five B-strokes (see page 9) to make the petals.

7. **Buds:** Paint the buds using the same method as the pansies' petals. Use a no. 4 flat shader to make only one B-stroke for each bud.

8. Dot the center of each pansy using a stylus and White. Use a no. 1 liner and Custard to pull two small comma strokes (see page 6) on either side of the White dot.

9. **Dots:** Randomly dot the space around the pansy area using the wooden end of the no. 1 liner and Butter Cream.

10. **Terra-cotta pots:** Paint the small pots Eucalyptus. Allow to dry. Dip the eraser end of a pencil in White paint and apply dots randomly to pots.

11. After the piece is dry, finish with two coats of Delta Satin Exterior/Interior Varnish. If desired, also apply a coat of varnish to the pots.

FRIEND'S JEWELRY BOX

If a friend enjoys collecting a variety of jewelry styles, she never has enough boxes for sorting and organizing her treasures. Of course, a beautiful, hand-painted jewel box from a close friend will always have a place of honor on top of her bureau.

This two-toned, weathered box has a charming aged appearance. The delightful painted images create a garden scene and set off a beautifully scripted sentiment highlighting the importance of friendship. How could she ever forget the special person who gave her this one-of-a-kind gift?

Periwinkle Blue

Custard

White

Eucalyptus

Dark Jungle Green

Ivory

Golden Brown

Burnt Sienna

FRIEND'S JEWELRY BOX

Supplies

Wooden box with lid
Delta All-Purpose Sealer
Delta Matte
  Exterior/Interior Varnish
Graphite paper, white
Sanding pad, fine grit
Stylus

Brushes

⅝-inch (15mm) flat shader
nos. 1, 2, 4, 6, 8, 10, 12 flat shaders
no. 4 round
nos. 1, 2 liners

Prep: Sand any rough edges using a fine grit sanding pad. Apply the sealer using a ⅝-inch (15mm) flat shader. Sand again to smooth the grain raised by the sealer.

1. Basecoat the entire box with Ivory and the ⅝-inch (15mm) flat shader.

2. Use Eucalyptus and the ⅝-inch (15mm) flat shader to dryly brush over the Ivory on the lid and band at the bottom of the box. Sand all the edges to give an aged appearance.

3. Transfer the pattern from page 43.

4. **Box border:** With a no. 1 liner and Burnt Sienna, paint a thin line around the top of the box as shown on pattern.

5. **Lettering:** Using a no. 1 flat shader and Burnt Sienna, stroke in all the lettering on the top of the box.

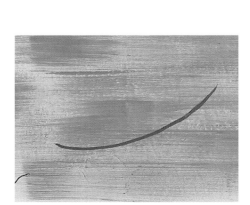

6. **Rose:** Double load a no. 10 flat shader with White and Ivory to create the rosebud using two C-strokes (see page 6) overlapping each other.

7. Stroke an S-stroke (see page 6) with the double-loaded brush over the two C-strokes.

8. Side load a no. 12 flat shader and float Golden Brown against the S-stroke on the rose and inside the throat. Side load a no. 12 flat shader with White to reinforce this float at the top stroke of the rose. Dot the throat using a stylus and White.

9. Using a no. 1 liner and a mix of Eucalyptus and Dark Jungle Green, stroke in the stems for the rose and daisies.

10. Use a double-loaded no. 8 flat shader with Eucalyptus and Dark Jungle Green to paint S-strokes for the four leaves under the rosebud.

11. **Comma strokes:** Double load a no. 2 liner by dragging one side through Eucalyptus and one side through Dark Jungle Green. Pull comma strokes (see page 6) at the base of the stem and above the rosebud.

12. **Daisies:** Use a no. 4 round brush and Ivory to stroke in the daisy petals. Use a no. 1 liner to line in the stem on the daisy using Dark Jungle Green.

13. Use Golden Brown and a no. 2 flat to base in the center of the daisy.

14. Side load a no. 8 flat shader with Burnt Sienna and float a C-stroke at the bottom of the center of the daisy.

15. With a no. 8 flat shader side loaded with Ivory, float a C-stroke along the top of the center of the daisy. Using a stylus and White, dot around the center of the daisy.

16. Mix Dark Jungle Green and Eucalyptus on a no. 2 liner and stroke in commas from the stem on the daisy in the lower left corner of the box.

17. **Butterfly:** Double load a no. 4 flat shader with Periwinkle Blue and White and stroke in the four closed C-strokes to create the butterfly.

18. Load a no. 1 liner with Burnt Sienna and stroke a tear drop (see page 7) for the body and two set downs (see page 7) for the antennae.

19. With the tip of the stylus, dot the butterfly wings with White.

20. **Leaves:** Double load a no. 6 flat shader with Dark Forest Green and Eucalyptus. Stroke in two two-stroke leaves (page 7) on the box front and two on the side of the box to form leaves.

21. Double load a no. 4 flat shader with Periwinkle Blue and White and stroke in five closed C-strokes to form each small flower.

22. Use the wooden end of a no. 1 liner to dot the center of all the blue flowers with Custard.

23. With the tip of the stylus and White, dot three groups of dots around the flowers.

24. Follow instructions in step 11 to stroke the comma strokes as shown on the pattern. Finish with a coat of varnish.

"BE HAPPY" TEA CADDY

Open the lid of this wooden box and you'll find little partitioned compartments, ideal for storing fancy tea bags. This is a perfect piece to paint and personalize for a friend

Surrounded by dainty bouquets, colorful china cups make it obvious this gift box is for a tea lover. Set off with a plaid border and sponged background, it's a lovely display box for the kitchen. If she's a true tea devotee, it's likely she already follows the charming, hand-lettered advice!

Gamal Green

 Village Green

 Sonoma Wine

 Dusty Mauve

 Cadet Grey

 Ivory

 White

 Blueberry

 Lavender Lace

 Straw

"BE HAPPY" TEA CADDY

Supplies

Wooden tea box (The Painting Goose)
Delta All-Purpose Sealer
Delta 14K Gold paint
Delta Exterior/Interior Varnish
Ruler and pencil
Sanding pad, fine grit
Stylus and graphite paper, gray
Sea sponge
1-inch (25mm) foam brush

Brushes

nos. 1, 6, 8, 12 flat shaders
no. 1 liner
no. 12 wave

Prep:

Sand any rough edges. Seal with Delta
All-Purpose Sealer using the 1-inch
(25mm) foam brush.

1. Basecoat the entire piece with Ivory and the 1-inch (25mm) foam brush.

2. Texture the box using a sea sponge and White. Pounce off the extra paint so that the stippling will be light and lacy.

3. Transfer the pattern from pages 44–45.

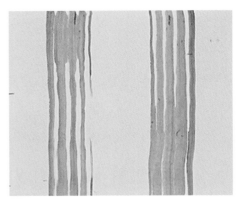

4. **Plaid:** Use a ruler and pencil to mark 1" (2.5cm) increments on the top and sides of the box. Load the no. 12 wave brush with Dusty Mauve thinned to an inky consistency and pull vertical lines at each pencil mark.

5. Also with the wave brush, use thinned Village Green to pull the horizontal lines.

6. Pull White lines with the wave brush above the green lines.

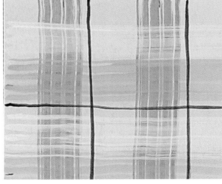

7. With the no. 1 liner and Gamal Green, pull a thin line on the bottom of the green wave lines.

8. Also with the no. 1 liner, pull a thin line of Sonoma Wine to the right of the vertical Dusty Mauve wave lines.

9. With the same liner, pull a diagonal White line from the Dusty Mauve vertical line to the Gamal Green line.

10. **Flowers:** Double load a no. 8 flat shader with White and Sonoma Wine. Paint closed C-strokes (see page 6) with the White toward the outer edge to create five-petal flowers in clusters in between the tea cups.

11. Use a no. 1 liner and White to create a starburst in the center of each flower. With the wooden end of the liner, add a dot of Dusty Mauve in the center of each starburst. Paint the flowers along the front of the tea holder in the same manner.

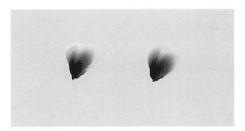

12. **Buds:** Double load a no. 6 flat shader with Sonoma Wine and White and paint a B-stroke (see page 7).

13. **Leaves:** Double load a no. 8 flat shader with Village Green and Gamal Green and paint two-stroke leaves (see page 7) around the flowers.

14. With a no. 1 liner and Gamal Green thinned to an inky consistency, stroke in the tendrils around all the flowers. Also pull stems to leaves and buds and stroke in calyx on buds.

15. **Lettering:** Stroke in the lettering (see page 8) using a no. 1 flat shader and Straw.

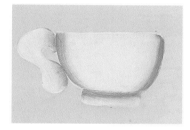

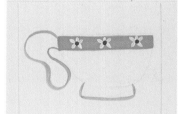

16. **Tea cups:** Basecoat the three tea cups using a no. 12 flat shader and White. Use a no. 12 flat shader and a side load of Cadet Grey to shade each cup where the handle joins the cup and along each side of the cup, angling off at the bottom. Also shade the base where it meets the cup.

Tea cup A: Use 14K Gold on a no. 6 flat shader to pull a curved band across the cup. With the no. 1 liner and 14K Gold, pull S-strokes (see page 6) along the top and bottom of the band and handle. Outline the handle and the top and bottom of the cup with 14K Gold.

Tea cup B: Use a no. 6 flat shader and Lavender Lace to pull flat stripes of color down to the bottom of the cup. With a no. 12 flat shader and Blueberry, float color on the outer edge of each lavender lace stripe. Thin 14K Gold to an inky consistency and with no. 1 liner, outline each side of the stripe and around the cup.

Tea cup C: Mix Dusty Mauve and White (1:1) and use a no. 6 flat shader to pull a line across the rim of the cup. Outline the handle and base using a no. 1 liner and the Dusty Mauve and White mix. Set down (see page 7) three small daisies using a no. 1 liner and White. Dot the center of each daisy using Dusty Mauve and a stylus. Finish with a coat of varnish.

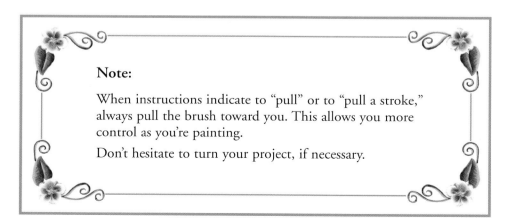

Note:

When instructions indicate to "pull" or to "pull a stroke," always pull the brush toward you. This allows you more control as you're painting.

Don't hesitate to turn your project, if necessary.

GUEST ROOM TRAY

Wooden trays are always a favorite among painters because they offer a good-sized, flat surface to decorate. Fortunately, trays are useful in so many different ways and they make a terrific gift idea. You can design a serving tray for tea, or create many types of gift ensembles using a painted tray as a container.

Painted in warm, rustic tones for old-fashioned flavor, this tray is a guest-bathroom gift for a visiting friend. It offers a welcoming message, revealed as she removes the collection of toiletries assembled for her benefit. There's no question—she'll "stay" as long as she can, and return as soon as possible!

Bahama Purple

Eucalyptus

Dark Jungle Green

Medium Flesh

Custard

Rose Petal Pink

Burnt Sienna

GUEST ROOM TRAY

Supplies

Small tray
Delta All-Purpose Sealer
Delta Matte Exterior/Interior
  Varnish
Stylus
Sanding pad, fine grit
Graphite paper, white
1-inch (25mm) foam brush

Brushes

nos. 2, 6, 16 flat shaders
no. 6 round
no. 1 liner

Prep:

Sand any rough edges using the fine grit sanding pad.
Use the 1-inch (25mm) foam brush to seal the tray.
Sand a second time to smooth any raised areas.

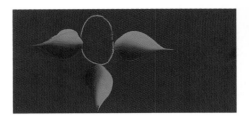

1. Basecoat the entire piece with Burnt Sienna and the 1-inch (25mm) foam brush.

2. Using a no. 16 flat shader and Bahama Purple, dryly brush the top edges of the tray. With a no. 1 liner and Bahama Purple, pull a thin line around the surface of the tray about ¼" (0.64 cm) in from each edge.

3. Transfer the pattern from page 46.

4. **Lettering:** Load a no. 2 flat shader with Custard and stroke in STAY (see page 8).

Paint the remainder of the lettering with a no. 1 liner and Custard.

5. **Leaves:** Double load a no. 6 flat with Eucalyptus and Dark Jungle Green. Stroke in three one-stroke leaves (see page 7).

6. **Rose:** Double load a no. 16 flat shader using Medium Flesh and Rose Petal Pink and stroke in the bowl of the rose using two C-strokes (see page 6).

7. With the no. 6 round double loaded with Medium Flesh and Rose Petal Pink, stroke in two comma strokes (see page 6) around the bowl of the rose to create the first two petals.

8. Stroke in two more petals.

9. Stroke in more petals as shown.

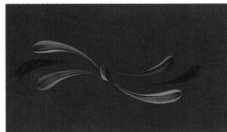

10. Side load a no. 16 flat shader with Medium Flesh and Burnt Sienna (1:1) and shade in the throat and bowl base of the rose. Dot the center of the rose with Custard using a stylus.

11. Use a no. 6 round to pull some comma strokes around the rose in Dark Jungle Green. Continue pulling the remainder of the strokes with a double-loaded brush of Dark Jungle Green and Eucalyptus.

12. **Small flowers:** Load a no. 1 liner with Bahama Purple and set down ovals (see page 7) to create blue flowers around the rose. Use a stylus and Custard to dot the centers of the flowers.

Side of tray: Refer to the photo and follow directions for the roses, leaves and small flowers.

13. Allow to dry, then brush on the varnish.

LOVE BLOOMS

Many people love these metal hanging vases that come in a wide variety of interesting shapes. Decorated and filled with a complementary bouquet, this project results in a unique piece of wall art and a great gift!

If your recipient loves a primitive, rustic look, you can leave some of the metal showing; otherwise coat the entire surface the way I have here. The two-toned paint helps call attention to the center design and charming, antique-style calligraphy. The lettering offers a lovely compliment to a special someone… "Wherever you go…love blooms."

Lavender
Lace

Bungalow
Blue

Chocolate
Cherry

Dark Foliage
Green

Light Foliage
Green

Dusty
Mauve

Pink Silk

LOVE BLOOMS

Supplies

Tin sconce (available from The Painting
    Goose)
Krylon Matte Spray
Delta Faux Finish Glaze Base, Clear
Graphite paper, white
1-inch (25mm) foam brush

Brushes

nos. 1, 2, 8, 12, 14 flat shaders
no. 1 liner
Scruffy brush

1. Prime the sconce with an application of matte spray. Allow to dry.

2. **Background:** Mix glaze and Lavender Lace (2:1). Paint the metal sconce with the mix using the 1-inch (25mm) foam brush.

3. Slip slap (see page 7) the area behind the rose pattern with a no. 14 flat shader and Bungalow Blue to darken slightly.

4. Trace on the pattern from page 42.

5. **Rose:** Basecoat the rose and buds with a mix of Pink Silk and Dusty Mauve (1:1) using a no. 14 flat shader. Re-trace the rose petals and bud lines using white graphite paper.

6. With a no. 12 flat shader and a side load of Dusty Mauve, add a float of color on the inside of the rose petals.

7. Use a no. 14 flat shader and Pink Silk to side load a float of color on the outer edges of the rose petals.

8. Stipple (see page 7) the center of the rose with Dusty Mauve using a scruffy brush.

9. **Rosebuds:** Use a no. 8 flat shader doubled loaded with Pink Silk and Dusty Mauve, then follow instructions on page 30 for a rosebud. Stipple as in step 8.

Leaves: Basecoat leaves with a mix of Dark and Light Foliage Greens (1:1) using a no. 14 flat shader. Side load a float of color at the base and bottom of each leaf using a no. 14 flat shader and Dark Foliage Green. With a no. 1 liner and Dark Foliage Green, paint S-strokes (see page 6) for veins in leaves.

10. Side load Dark Foliage Green on a no. 2 flat shader and float the color where the stem attaches to the rose and behind the cut edge. Side load a float of Light Foliage Green on the top edge of each leaf using a no. 14 flat shader.

11. **Lettering:** Use a no. 1 flat shader flattened and Chocolate Cherry to paint the lettering (see page 8). Finish with a coat of Krylon Matte Spray.

Wherever You Go...

Love Blooms

Page 40

Side of Planter

Sow so

Page 26

Page 26

Friends are the
jewels of life

Front of Jewlery Box Page 29

Page 29

eds of kindness

I made a wish and you came true

Page 22

be happy with simple ple

Page 33

Every day is a Gift

Page 19

'Tis Always Morning Somewhere

asures

to Unfold

Front of Box Page 33

Page 16

Seize the day Page 13

Side of Tray Page 37

Stay Page 37

is a lovely word
in a friend's vocabulary

PAINT CONVERSION CHART

Ceramcoat by Delta	Americana™ by DecoArt	Folk Art® by Plaid
Autumn Brown 2005	Light Cinnamon	Nutmeg/Maple Syrup+Brown Sugar 1:1
Bahama Purple 2518	Country Blue+Orchid 1:1	White+Purple Lilac+Cobalt Blue 5:1:1
Bambi Brown 2424	Mink Tan	Mushroom
Blueberry 2513	Wedgewood Blue	Thunder Blue+White 6:1
Blue Wisp 2455	Blue Mist	Summer Sky+Light Grey+White 2:1:1
Bungalow Blue 2575	Country Blue+French Grey Blue+Blue Violet 2:1:1	Sterling Blue+Baby Blue 2:1
Burnt Sienna 2030	Light Cinnamon+Russet 3:1	Light Red Oxide+Burnt Sienna 2:1
Butter Cream 2523	Light Buttermilk+Buttermilk 1:1	Warm White+Taffy 1:1
Cadet Grey 2426	Neutral Grey Toning+Buttermilk 2:1	Light Grey+Dapple Grey 5:1
Cape Cod Blue 2133	French Grey/Blue	Settler's Blue
Charcoal 2436	Graphite	Charcoal Grey+Black 4:1
Custard 2448	Taffy Cream	Lemonade
Dark Foliage Green 2535	Hauser Dark Green+Deep Teal 1:1	Hauser Green Dark (AP)
Dark Forest Green 2096	Evergreen+Plantation Pine 1:1	Thicket
Dark Jungle Green 2420	Evergreen	Olive Green
Deep Lilac 2577	Dioxazine Purple+Cadmium Red (T)	Violet Pansy
Dusty Mauve 2405	Antique Mauve	Rose Garden
Eggplant 2486	Dioxazne Purple+True Red 2:1	Red Violet
Eucalyptus 2569	Hauser Medium Green+Celery Green 1:1	Hauser MediumGreen+Bayberry+Medium Grey 1:1:1
Forest Green 2010	Avocado+Evergreen 2:1	Old Ivy
Gamal Green 2120	Plantation Pine	Olive Green+Dark Grey 3:1
Golden Brown 2054	Honey Brown	English Mustard
Ivory 2036	Sand (L)	Taffy (L)
Lavender 2047	Lavender+Neutral Grey 3:1	Purple Lilac
Lavender Lace 2016	Flesh+Country Blue 3:1	Cotton Candy+Porcelain Blue 1:1
Light Foliage Green 2537	Hauser Light Green	Hauser Light Green (AP)
Light Ivory 2401	Light Buttermilk	Warm White (AP)
Magnolia White 2487	White Wash	Wicker White
Medium Flesh 2126	Medium Flesh	Skintone+Georgia Peach 2:1
Medium Foliage Green 2536	Hauser Medium Green	Hauser Medium Green (AP)
Moss Green 2570	Desert Sand+Jade 3:1	Basil Green+White 1:1
Old Parchment 2092	Moon Yellow	Sunflower+Buttercup 3:1
Pale Lilac 2576	Orchid+Lavender+White 4:1:1	Ballet Pink+Heather 4:1
Payne's Grey 2512	Payne's Grey	Payne's Grey+Prussian Blue (T)
Periwinkle Blue 2478	Country Blue	Light Periwinkle
Phthalo Blue 2502	Primary Blue	True Blue
Pink Silk 2566	HiLite Flesh+Pink Chiffon 2:1	White+Strawberry Parfait 4:T
Purple Dusk 2522	Country Blue+Dioxazine Purple 3:1	Periwinkle+Purple Lilac 2:1
Rhythm 'N Blue 2551	Blue Violet+Dioxazine Purple 3:1	Brilliant Blue+Night Sky 4:1
Rose Petal Pink 2521	Pink Chiffon	White+Ballet Pink 1:1
Salem Blue 2121	Salem Blue+Buttermilk 2:1	Azure Blue+Buttercream 1:1
Sonoma Wine 2446	Rookwood Red	Huckleberry+Burnt Sienna 1:1
Spice Brown 2049	Milk Chocolate	Nutmeg
Stonewedge Green 2442	Celery Green	Basil Green+Southern Pine 6:1
Straw 2078	Golden Straw	Buttercup
Village Green 2447	Jade Green+White 1:1	Poetry Green+White 1:1
Vintage Wine 2434	Royal Purple	Midnight Violet
Wedgwood Green 2070	Jade Green	Bayberry
White 2505	White (Snow or Titanium)	White (Titanium) AP

D - Darker   L - Lighter   T - Touch   AP - Artist's Pigment

Explore the world of decorative painting with North Light Books!

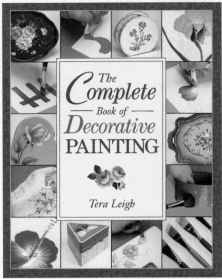

These books and other fine North Light titles are available from your local art & craft retailer, bookstore, online supplier or by calling 1-800-448-0915.

This book is the must-have one-stop reference for decorative painters, crafters, home decorators and do-it-yourselfers. It's packed with solutions to every painting challenge, including surface preparation, lettering, borders, faux finishes, strokework techniques and more! You'll also find five fun-to-paint projects designed to instruct, challenge and entertain you—no matter what your skill level.

ISBN 1-58180-062-2, paperback, 256 pages, #31803-K

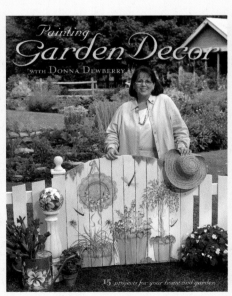

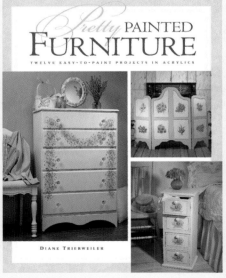

Transform your everyday outdoor furnishings into stunning, hand-painted garden accents. Acclaimed decorative painter Donna Dewberry shows you how to transform 15 deck, porch and patio pieces into truly lovely garden décor. Donna's easy-to-master brushwork techniques make each one fun and rewarding. No green thumb required!

ISBN 1-58180-144-0, paperback, 144 pages, #31889-K

Learn to paint your favorite Christmas themes, including Santas, angels, elves and more, on everything from glittering ornaments to festive albums. Renowned decorative painter John Gutcher shows you how with 9 all-new, step-by-step projects. He makes mastering tricky details simple with special tips for painting fur, hair, richly textured clothing and realistic flesh tones.

ISBN 1-58180-105-X, paperback, 128 pages, #31794-K

Add beauty and elegance to every room in your home! Diane Trierweiler makes it easy with step-by-step instructions for giving old furniture a facelift and new furniture a personal touch. You'll learn how to paint everything from berries to butterflies on chests, chairs and more. Includes 12 complete projects with color charts and traceable patterns.

ISBN 1-58180-234-X, paperback, 128 pages, #32009-K